Original title:
Threads of Tomorrow

Copyright © 2025 Creative Arts Management OÜ
All rights reserved.

Author: Lila Davenport
ISBN HARDBACK: 978-1-80586-156-0
ISBN PAPERBACK: 978-1-80586-628-2

Ties of Hope

In a world spun from giggles and dreams,
The silly knots fray at the seams,
Tangled in laughter, we spin and we dance,
Wobbling forward, we take a chance.

Socks mismatched, shoes on the wrong feet,
Chasing our worries, oh, what a feat!
Falling with grace, we stifle a snort,
Every misstep, a jolly report.

With half-baked ideas, we start to collide,
Planning adventures, at least we're not fried,
Home-made helmets from tin foil nearby,
Victory laps in pajamas, oh my!

From balloons to cookies, our hopes are so spry,
Each chuckle a ladder to reach for the sky,
Building our futures with send-ups and puns,
In our playful kingdom, we're all silly buns.

A Mosaic of Promised Dawns

In the chaos of dawn, coffee spills,
Mugs try to dance, but trip on hills.
The sun peeks in, with a grinning face,
And all our plans just pick up pace.

Jelly beans bounce on the kitchen floor,
They plot a heist, then demand much more.
Tickles of laughter, we spill on the night,
As daybreak paints everything so bright.

Ties that Bind Across Time

A sock escapes to play hide and seek,
It floats like a cloud, oh what a freak!
Time machines built from cardboard and tape,
Flying to lunches, oh what a shape!

We hop on bikes, like time travel's best,
Wobbling and giggling, we forget the rest.
A sandwich flies, like it's on a quest,
While crumbs plot schemes, in a crummy jest.

The Starlit Loom of Possibility

Under the stars, where pizza dreams fly,
Aliens order, but they don't comply.
They giggle and dance in glittery shoes,
Making new flavors of cosmic snooze.

With marshmallow planets, and soda streams,
Ideas drift off, like sweet summer dreams.
But cats take the stage, asserting their reign,
With tails like comets, they cause such a strain.

Threads Intertwined with Destiny

Banana peels on the sidewalks lay,
Waiting to catch someone in mid-play.
Fortunes told by squirrels on the fence,
With accents that make zero sense!

The hammock sways with a breezy tune,
As fish start dreaming of flying to the moon.
Life's little quirks make us laugh and twirl,
As we weave bright stories in a silly whirl.

Connecting Moments

In the cafe, I spilled my tea,
A cat jumped up, just to see.
He danced a jig, all in a rush,
As my muffin became a mush.

A squirrel stole my sandwich too,
He waved goodbye with a chipmunk crew.
I laughed so hard, I lost my hat,
As they scampered off, cheeky and fat.

New Stitches in Time

I took up knitting, oh what a sight,
Endless loops tangled all night.
The yarn escaped like a cheeky mouse,
My blanket's now a woolly house.

With needles clashing, a symphony loud,
My cat danced around, oh so proud.
A scarf turned into a bouncy ball,
Next thing I know, I'm in a yarn brawl!

Woven Realities

In my dreams, I tried to weave,
A tapestry of what to believe.
Instead, I stitched a silly face,
With googly eyes and a furry lace.

I thought I'd make a cloak of grace,
But ended up with a llama's embrace.
Now everyone asks where it's from,
I just say it's the latest fashion, yum!

Imagined Patterns

My plans were drawn with great finesse,
A maze of colors, I must confess.
But when I looked, all was a blur,
A rainbow snake, without a spur.

I set out bold to plant some seeds,
But grew a jungle of funny weeds.
They giggled as they took the sun,
"Oh dear," I thought, "this ain't much fun!

Hues of Tomorrow

In a world where socks go missing,
Colors clash, oh what a dissing.
Bright yellows and greens they dance,
Fashion trends lost in a trance.

Mismatched shoes tell a tale,
Of ludicrous winds that prevail.
Hats that wobble, wigs that fly,
To the style police, oh my, oh my!

A Continuum Unraveled

The laundry monster lurks at night,
Stealing clothes, what a fright!
One day you're chic, the next a mess,
Fashion's game is such a stress.

Every closet feels like a jumble,
With skirts and pants that just stumble.
Ever try socks for a hat?
On Mondays? That's where it's at!

New Threads of Life

Life wraps us up like an old quilt,
With crazed patterns, accidentally built.
Button down, or let it sway,
Who knew laundry could play this way?

A new shirt claims it's all the rage,
But feels more like a fashion cage.
If stripes and polka dots can kiss,
Oh, what a bold experiment, right? Bliss!

The Artisan's Proposition

An artisan juggled fabric scraps,
Crafting wonders, perhaps mishaps.
A dress from ties? A coat from jeans?
Creative chaos reigns in dreams!

Stitch by stitch, laughter in seams,
Patterns born from wildest schemes.
So grab your scissors, don't delay,
Fashion whimsies are here to stay!

Looming Visions of What's to Come

In the corner, clowns await,
Juggling dreams, but never late.
A cat in boots ties up a plan,
To fly a kite with a frying pan.

Unicorns on roller skates,
Inviting us to silly fates.
A toast to those who dance on clouds,
With mustached fish that swim in crowds.

Fabric of Hope Woven Tight

A toaster sings a cheerful tune,
While socks debate the shape of June.
Paper planes dive with a quack,
As jellybeams launch from the snack.

Underwear in a dapper suit,
Hit the town on a bright pink flute.
With every stitch, a giggle grows,
As marshmallow men do the tango.

Pathways Sewn from Starlight

A jellybean road, oh what a sight,
Where gummy bears dance, day and night.
Shooting stars play hopscotch too,
On paths of paint that smell like dew.

Popcorn clouds float way up high,
With laughter that tickles the sky.
Skittles rain down, a sweet delight,
As cupcakes plan their moonlit flight.

The Weave of Unwritten Days

Frogs in bow ties croak a cheer,
As we embrace the comic year.
With floppy hats, they skip and prance,
In a grand masquerade of chance.

A penguin winks, it's all a joke,
In a world where laughter's bespoke.
With every twist, a quirky play,
We'll laugh our way through each new day.

New Embroideries

In a world where socks don't match,
A painter spills his big old stash.
The kittens dance in threads so bright,
While we just hope that pants fit right.

A yo-yo ties the days in knots,
Juggling dreams like chicken pots.
Mismatched shoes, a clownish feat,
Laughing as we shuffle our feet.

Funny hats parade around,
While jellybeans are lost and found.
Ink from pens that never dry,
Create the scribbles, oh my, oh my!

So let's embroider quirks galore,
And open wide the silly door.
With laughter's thread we'll stitch our fate,
In this grand life we celebrate.

Unraveling Hopes

The cat is plotting with a grin,
His yarn ball soon is deemed a win.
As socks disappear without a trace,
We wonder who will take their place.

A parade of mismatched drawers,
Who knew lost clothes could start some wars?
With every snag and every twist,
Our hopes unravel, but don't be missed!

Tangled dreams in a knotted mess,
The toaster mutters, 'I must confess.'
Popcorn ceilings springing up high,
As dreams bounce like a spring chicken fly.

So laugh a little at the absurd,
In hopes that all the chaos heard.
With every loop and curve we make,
We find the joy in every break.

Illuminated Pathways

In a land of socks that shine like stars,
A rubber chicken brews up avatars.
With spaghetti roads and marshmallow trees,
We giggle and chortle with joy and ease.

The light bulbs dance with glee in their spheres,
While cupcakes ride on bicycles, cheers!
Twirling in laughter, we bounce and sway,
On this illuminated, silly pathway.

A parrot sings tunes of lost remote,
While bicycles float and play boat.
Being silly is what we seek,
On this road, it's fun that speaks!

So come and join the dreamy spree,
Where happiness flows like hot green tea.
In this bright land where laughter's free,
We'll dance through life, just you and me.

The Loom of Tomorrow

In a loom where hopes are wound so tight,
Frogs in bow ties leap with delight.
With every weave, a giggle escapes,
As rubber ducks wear funny capes.

The clock strikes twelve—oh what a sight!
A snail in sneakers zips left and right.
With strands of laughter all around,
In this whimsical world, joy is found.

Tangled tales of socks that pair,
With unicorns dancing without a care.
While spaghetti swirls ride on the breeze,
Laughter is sewn with the greatest of ease.

So gather 'round for the chuckles we share,
In the loom of tomorrow, there's fun everywhere.
With a wink and a smile, we'll forever create,
This tapestry of joy—we won't hesitate!

Quiet Threads of Change

In the corner sat a cat,
With a hat that looked quite flat.
He plotted schemes of great delight,
To change the world by morning light.

He chased the mice with silly prance,
While wearing socks, a funny chance.
The dog just wagged and gave a grin,
Let's see what trouble they begin!

The goldfish had a dream one day,
To run a race—oh, what a play!
With fins he'd fly and jump so high,
They laughed along, oh me, oh my!

So laugh, dear friend, at all these quirks,
For change is fun, it's never jerks.
In cat and dog, and fish, we see,
The world is wild, and that's the key!

Beyond the Horizon

A chicken once believed it could,
Fly past the fence, oh yes, it would!
With feathers fluffed and wings wide spread,
It launched, but landed on its head.

An old goat cheered from the hilltop,
Moo, he thought, what a funny flop!
Yet every laugh rang out with joy,
For dreams, it seems, bring silly ploy!

Across the fields, a rumor grew,
Of flying beasts no one knew.
So cow and hen drew up a scheme,
To start a farm with a dream team!

With jokes and jests, they'd build their way,
Beyond the fence, they'd laugh and play.
As laughter echoed 'gainst the sky,
Together they would surely fly!

Intertwined Futures

In a town where socks went missing,
The residents had dreams worth kissing.
They formed a club; oh, what a sight,
To find their socks and win the night!

With clever traps made out of yarn,
They waited there, a comic swarm.
The poodles draped in scarves so bright,
Said, "Let's have fun till morning light!"

A box appeared and out came shoes,
But socks? They'd only find the blues.
Yet laughter rang from door to door,
As mismatched pairs danced on the floor!

So join this quest that leads to cheer,
Where socks may vanish, but friends are near.
With giggles loud and socks askew,
The futures bright when shared with you!

Silken Aspirations

In a garden where the plants converse,
A lilac dreamed of fame, of course!
It practiced poses 'neath the sun,
To be the pretty one, that's fun!

A dandelion blew seeds around,
Said, "I'll be famous underground!"
The roots beneath would cheer and shout,
Just wait and see what I'm about!

A sunflower chimed in with flair,
"I'll stand up straight without a care!"
They plotted out their big debut,
The garden show, what a hullabaloo!

When time did come to show their art,
They danced and twirled, each played a part.
With laughter bright and colors bold,
In every petal, dreams untold!

Fragments of the Future

In a world of mismatched shoes,
Dance steps found in yesterday's news.
Cats wear hats, oh what a sight,
Pigeons gossip in broad daylight.

Chickens dream of flying high,
While squirrels plot their sneaky spy.
Bananas dress in polka dots,
In a kitchen where chaos never stops.

Aliens hover, sipping tea,
Fixing Earth's broken GPS spree.
Jellybeans float on clouds of cream,
In a land where nothing's as it seems.

So grab your socks and skip a beat,
Life's a quirky, silly treat.
Tomorrow's waiting, don't you fret,
With laughter, there's no regret.

Tapestry of Hope

Socks unmatched, but full of glee,
A tapestry of silliness, can't you see?
Unicorns bake cakes that fizz,
And frogs sit playing jazz, like whiz!

Cupcakes wear sprinkles like a crown,
While jellyfish roam the town.
Dogs in suits debate the news,
And mice in glasses mold fresh views.

The sun winks brightly, dressed in gold,
With stories of laughter yet untold.
Rainbows grow like wildflowers,
In the garden of brave dreamers' powers.

Hope sprouts wings, takes off in flight,
Chasing giggles, shining bright.
Life's patchwork, stitched with cheer,
A dance of joy, calling us near.

Echoes of Dawn

As dawn arrives with a silly grin,
Waking the world with a gentle spin.
Roosters play jazz, strut their stuff,
While coffee beans call, "We're not enough!"

Cereal boxes dance and jive,
With spoons and milk, they feel alive.
The sun tickles the sleepy moon,
As bunnies bounce to their own tune.

Winds whisper secrets of the day,
Socks with polka dots come out to play.
Kittens chase their tails in a loop,
Creating quite the fancy troupe.

Laughter echoes, ringing clear,
Filling hearts with cheer and beer.
A whimsical start to life's parade,
In the joyful mess, dreams are made.

Weaving Whispers

Whispers of giggles float through the air,
Weaving stories with mischief to share.
Toasters sing tunes as they pop,
While crazy squirrels act like they're hot!

Frogs in bowties hop with flair,
Debating fashion, they don't care.
A picnic spread with jellybeans,
Where ants run fashion shows with jeans.

Clouds wear hats, it's quite the scene,
Dragons sip tea from a bottle green.
Time giggles, twisting like a vine,
Promising laughter, oh how divine!

So join the dance, embrace the cheer,
Life's a party, have no fear.
With every whisper, new tales arise,
In a world where laughter never dies.

Strands of Possibility

Twisting and turning in a cosmic dance,
Spaghetti and meatballs, what a strange chance!
Fingers get tangled in webs of delight,
Life's a big mess, but oh, what a sight!

Puppies are running with socks on their heads,
While grandpa is misplacing his teeth in his beds.
Juggling bananas with monkeys all around,
Who knew such chaos could be so profound?

Let's paint the sky with colors so bold,
While the cat plays violin in a coat made of gold.
Chasing the sunshine in mismatched shoes,
Dancing on rooftops with nothing to lose!

So here's to the giggles and slips on the floor,
Life's just a carnival, who could ask for more?
Celebrate moments that make you burst,
In this carnival of life, we are forever immersed!

Pathways Unraveled

Walking the tightrope on stilts of good cheer,
While tripping on gummi bears, oh dear, oh dear!
Plotting the path like a curious squirrel,
Every corner reveals a new twist and twirl!

Tangled in shoelaces, trying to flee,
But clumsy old me just fell into a tree.
Who knew those branches would be so inviting?
Now I'm just a fruitcake, flipping and fighting!

The ducks are quacking in synchronized time,
While I'm dancing awkwardly, utterly sublime.
Swapping stories with creatures of lore,
In this whimsical world, who could ask for more?

With candy-coated clouds and jellybean skies,
Let's weave our way through a realm of surprise.
Hand in hand, we embrace every stumble,
Finding joy in the chaos, let's laugh and rumble!

Tides of Change

Riding the waves on a surfboard of cheese,
Laughing with dolphins who dance in the breeze.
The ocean's a punchline, a joke on the shore,
Where crabs hold auditions for musicals galore!

Seagulls are critiquing my style and my flair,
As I splash in the water, without any care.
Flip-flops a-flopping, what a glorious sight,
We're the kings and the queens of this fanciful night!

With seashell confetti and starfish in tow,
We'll ride out the waves wherever they go.
Life's like a carnival, splashes and spins,
With laughter like bubbles, the fun never thins!

So let's catch the rhythm of waves as they sway,
In this goofy adventure, come what may.
Together we'll glide through the whirlpool of fate,
In the ocean of giggles, we truly create!

Embroidered Journeys

Stitching together the tales that we weave,
With colors that pop like a bright autumn leave.
Every patch tells a story, a quirky design,
In this quilt of adventures, we're feeling just fine!

Knitting together our laughs and our dreams,
With yarn made of jellybeans bursting at seams.
As we thread through the chaos of life's wacky spree,
A tapestry woven with moments of glee!

Button-eyed monsters join in the fun,
As we chase after sunsets and race with the sun.
Sewing our futures with glitter and glue,
In this whimsical world, there's so much to do!

So paint us a picture with threads made of cheer,
In this fabric of laughter, there's nothing to fear.
Together we'll journey through shirts that may fray,
But loving the colors, come what may!

Fables Yet to Be

In a world where socks all roam,
Lost from pairs, they seek a home.
A t-shirt dreams of days ahead,
To fly and dance, not just be thread.

A cape that thinks it's meant for flight,
Craves adventure by moonlight.
A scarf with stories, twists and bends,
Giggles with buttons, old time friends.

The pants, they swear, plan to escape,
While hats just ponder, 'What's my shape?'
All these fables whisper clear,
Tomorrow's laughter draws so near.

Fabrics of Time

In the cupboard, dust bunnies plot,
To weave a tale that's quite a lot.
Old jeans reminisce about the dance,
While aprons conspire in a sewing romance.

A button rolls, claiming to be sage,
As patches tell of every age.
A blanket craves a wild parade,
With funky socks that never fade.

Each fragment dreams of cosmic swings,
Hoping to play the cosmic strings.
In laughing colors, they unite,
Woven fabric spun from might.

Echoing Possibilities

A bowtie dreams of fancy balls,
While dust rags whisper through the halls.
A pair of gloves, with mismatched flair,
Tickle each other, 'Do we dare?'

In the closet, shoes exchange winks,
Plotting dances, giddy blinks.
While old hats ponder who'll wear them next,
Creating tales, weirdly perplexed.

Eager scarves spin tales of glee,
Gazing at pockets, oh so free.
In this playful, fabric-filled space,
Echoes of joy embrace the place.

The Loom of Life

In the loom where odd socks meet,
They stitch together a rhythmic beat.
A bow insists it's quite the star,
While laces boast, 'We've come so far!'

The quilt debates the best of styles,
As borders tease and bind with smiles.
Every fabric holds a sign,
'Let's mix and match, it'll be divine!'

With every twist and playful turn,
The threads of laughter brightly churn.
A patchwork life that's simply fun,
Weaving the smiles, we've just begun.

Threads of Tomorrow's Echo

In the sewing room of fate, we laugh,
Stitching dreams with quirky craft,
Buttons dancing, zippers flip,
A fabric party, what a trip!

Socks protesting, their colors clash,
One sock's missing, what a splash!
Hats wobble, it's a zany show,
We weave our futures, row by row!

Needles prickle with silly cheer,
As we thread hopes without any fear,
Patterns that twist, then hilariously bend,
In this fabric world, we won't pretend!

So let's patch the holes in our plans,
With laughter sewn into our hands,
For in this chaos; we gleefully spin,
All the fun starts where we begin!

Fabricating Dreams

Sewing dreams with threads of glee,
Stitches hopping like a bumblebee,
Yarn balls rolling all around,
In this fabric fun, joy is found!

Buttons giggle, they play peek-a-boo,
While the scissors snip to the morning dew,
Patterns jive, so wild and free,
Creating tales of whimsy, you see!

Measuring smiles in yards and inches,
As laughter rips through paradoxes,
Quilting wishes with a funny sway,
Sew what if we're lost on the way?

A patchwork life, a comical ride,
In every fiber, a grin applied,
Let's fabricate a future quite bright,
With stitches of joy, take-off in flight!

The Times We Forge

In the forge of giggles, ideas collide,
With hammers of humor, we take pride,
Duct tape dreams and bright cardboard flames,
We twist our fate into silly games!

Time ticks funny as we craft and create,
A sandwich with glitter? We can't wait!
A future of jellybeans, oh what a sight,
Who knew odd inventions could feel so right?

Forging laughter with every swing,
In a world where nonsense is king,
Jokes hammered in between each beat,
Our future's a dance, isn't that neat?

So gather your tools, come take a chance,
Join the fun, let your dreams dance,
For in the times we play and explore,
We'll forge tomorrow, always wanting more!

Destiny's Fabric

In the fabric shop of fate's embrace,
We cut and sew with smiles on our face,
Threading giggles into each seam,
Patchwork lives—what a dream team!

Clothespins dance like they know the score,
As fabric sways, calling for more,
With each snip, our mischief unfurls,
Woven tales in a world of twirls!

A tapestry bright, with quirks galore,
Laughter stitched in, who could ask for more?
Destiny laughs, a chuckle so bold,
As we weave our paths in threads of gold!

So grab your yarn, let's play a tune,
Under the sun, or beneath the moon,
For in this fabric, we find our art,
Laughter and love are the best part!

Patterned Visions of Unseen Worlds

In a closet full of socks,
A derby hat starts to box.
A cat in boots, ready to dance,
Believes it's got the best chance.

A fish in shades swims with flair,
Waves to the fridge, free as air.
While bread loaves dream of toast skies,
As peanut butter plots its rise.

A couch tells tales of lost remote,
A playful ghost in a candy coat.
Televisions chuckle and hum,
At all the lives that they welcome and numb.

So let's spin yarn from every giggle,
And knit a world that makes us wiggle.
For in this mesh of jolly scenes,
Reality's funnier than it seems!

Journey Crafted in the Loom of Now.

A snail on a skateboard rolls by,
Waving at pigeons that fly high.
Rabbits in sneakers chase their tails,
While turtles decide on epic trails.

The clock ticks backward, what a sight,
As shadows dance with pure delight.
A frog plays chess with a wise old bee,
Debating the merits of sweet vs. tea.

With every stitch of laughter sewn,
We craft adventures yet unknown.
In the fabric of the here and now,
Let's turn the mundane to a wow!

So humor blossoms in every thread,
As we weave our stories, well-fed.
In this tapestry of cheer and play,
Unseen worlds come out to stay!

Woven Dreams

A dreamer knits with colors bright,
Casting spells by candlelight.
Buttons twinkle, stars in a jar,
As cupcakes dance beneath the stars.

A squirrel in a hat reads a book,
While cookies bake with a secret look.
A plant whispers oh-so-softly sweet,
Inviting ants to join for a treat.

With every stitch, a chuckle grows,
As silly stories beg to be prose.
In the laughter of breezy air,
Our woven dreams become the rare.

So grab your yarn, and join the spree,
Let's craft a world where we feel free.
In fabric woven, joy unfolds,
With whimsy stitching stories bold!

Stitches of Fate

A pencil decided to play with glue,
While socks conspired to start a coup.
Bubbles giggled with laughter bright,
In a circus hat, ready for flight.

A rubber duck held a serious chat,
With a sleepy cat and a mischievous rat.
Together they plotted an escape plan,
To ride the waves like a rockstar band.

In each stitch, fate twirls around,
As silly antics abound in sound.
The ordinary hides a funny fate,
That dances lightly and won't hesitate.

So let's bend the rules and have some fun,
With stitches that sparkle, every one.
In the fabric of life, let's play our part,
With a heart full of laughter and a joyous art!

Weaving Light into the Shadows

In the loom of night, we play,
With colors bright, we chase the gray.
A stitch of giggles, a knot of cheer,
We dance with laughter, no room for fear.

Tangled yarns of dreams collide,
As we juggle visions, laughter as our guide.
A patchwork quilt of silly scenes,
Painting futures in vibrant sheens.

With each loop, we spin a tale,
Of cats in hats and fish that sail.
The threads of joy, a vibrant throng,
In this funny weave, we all belong.

So grab a needle, thread it right,
Let's stitch together this quirky night!
With every chuckle, we sew anew,
Creating a canvas, just me and you.

The Footfalls of Future Dreams

Tiptoe through the puddles bright,
Where dreams bounce high and take to flight.
With squeaky shoes and a playful leap,
We chase tomorrow, no time for sleep.

In every hop, a giggle spills,
As we navigate through joy-filled hills.
Skimming stones on a laughing stream,
Each ripple whispers, 'Chase your dream!'

Future paths are paved in fun,
With jellybeans beneath the sun.
We strut along, with a silly sway,
Collecting giggles along the way.

So let's bumble down this crazy lane,
With footsteps wild that dance like rain.
We will leap, we will bound,
In these charming dreams, joy is found.

Woven Whispers of Hope and Change

In a garden of giggles, flowers bloom,
With buzzing bees and a joyful tune.
Whispers float on a breezy sigh,
As butterflies wink and pass us by.

Every hope's a sprout, taking a chance,
Laughing at leaves in a playful dance.
The winds of change, a ticklish breeze,
Are tickling the branches of giggling trees.

We sow the seeds of dreams in jest,
Bouncing ideas like a conga fest.
With every chuckle, new blooms appear,
In this silly journey, we hold so dear.

So let's weave wishes, one by one,
With laughter knitting 'til the day is done.
For in every smile, hope takes its flight,
Woven whispers basking in light.

Intricacies of a Shimmering Path

On a path of sparkles, we wander wide,
With giggles glimmering, side by side.
Each step we take, a silly twirl,
As we chase rainbows that sway and swirl.

With every pebble, a chuckle brings,
Funky dances and makeshift swings.
We skip through puddles, splash with glee,
In this dazzling journey, just you and me.

A path lined with wishes and tinkling chimes,
Every turn tells tales, infused with rhymes.
With whimsy leading, we boldly roam,
Finding the laughter that feels like home.

So tie your shoes, let's hit the road,
As we piece together every joyful ode.
Intricacies shaped in colors bright,
On this shimmering adventure, we take flight.

Evolving Designs

In a world that's always shifting,
We stitch our hopes with laughter,
Designs that twist and turn like dandelions,
With every misstep, we happily chase after.

A zipper here, a button there,
Fashion faux pas, we wear with flair,
Add a splash of paint, it's quite a sight,
If we can't look good, we'll surely delight.

Socks don't match, but who really cares?
A rogue with style, avoiding stares,
The color wheel is spinning fast,
A kaleidoscope of fun we cast.

Each outfit tells a tale of glee,
As we dance through life's grand spree,
So grab your tape, your active glue,
Evolving styles, we make our debut.

Harvesting Dreams

In fields of wishes, we gather cheer,
Planting giggles, spreading good cheer,
With every seed, a laugh we sow,
Harvesting joy, it's quite the show.

A pumpkin rolls, it slips on cue,
Off to the market, we bid adieu,
Carving out smiles with knives that gleam,
We're not just farmers, we're living the dream.

The corn stalks sway, a dance so grand,
With chickens clucking, and goats that stand,
Maybe we'll raise a silly parade,
Harvesting laughter, our grand charade.

Each bucket full of quirky surprise,
In this garden of laughter, joy never dies,
We'll bake it in pies, or wear it like cream,
Life's delicious when we're harvesting dreams.

Silhouettes of the Future

Shadows dancing on the lunar ground,
Funny figures echoing sound,
Aliens twirling with galactic style,
We laugh 'til we drop, there's no denial.

Futuristic hats that hover and spin,
Dodging the laser beams, we grin,
With robots serving us ice cream treats,
Who needs a manual when life's so sweet?

Flying cars, they zoom and crash,
But life is good in this noodle mash,
Every mishap brings another grin,
In the silliness, we'll always win.

So let's embrace the unknown play,
With every silhouette found on display,
The future's a canvas, wild and bright,
A laughter-filled path, a joyful flight.

Ties that Bind

In knots and bows, our laughter's twined,
With silly ties that warp the mind,
Each meeting feels like a carnival fair,
With every quirk, we make the square.

Tangled strings, a jumble of fun,
Who knew a knotted pull could run?
We stumble and giggle, such a delight,
Ties that bind us to the night.

Grandpa's suspenders take flight,
As grandma's cackle ignites the night,
We weave our tales with yarns so bright,
In threads of laughter, we find our light.

So raise a toast to the goofy crew,
With ties that twist and hearts so true,
Let's bind our joy, a comical tune,
With every chuckle, we'll soar like a balloon.

Fragile Connections

In a web spun from bristles and yarn,
A cat ponders his next grand plan.
He swipes at a spool, oh what a mess,
Turns a neat room to a crafty distress.

A button lost, a sock in disguise,
Each piece of fabric, a tale in the skies.
Mom's sewing kit, my treasure trove,
Where half-finished projects dance and strove.

Laughter echoes through colors that blend,
Patchwork creations that never quite mend.
A hiccup, a snicker, a snort slightly loud,
In the land of mishaps, I'm wonderfully proud.

So here's to the chaos that weaving presents,
Where errors become our comical events.
A string here, a knot there, laughter won't stop,
In this merry mess, we giggle and hop.

Sketching the Unseen

On a canvas of paper, a doodle ignites,
A creature composed of spaghetti delights.
Eyes made of buttons, a nose like a shoe,
Artistry's charm is a sight, oh, who knew?

Pencil's gone wild, it circles and twirls,
Drawing new worlds amidst giggles and swirls.
Each line's a mishap, but isn't it fun?
Sketching the unseen, my creative run.

A duck wears a hat that's five sizes too big,
While a bear in a tutu takes the stage, oh so sprig!
With laughter, we paint prankish plans on the page,
In the gallery of giggles, we artfully engage.

My sketches may wobble, but silly they sing,
An unseen world born from a wild doodling fling.
So grab your pencil, let nonsense unfold,
Create with abandon; let humor take hold.

Vibrant Futures

In a land where socks don't quite match,
And mismatched shoes play a silly catch.
A rainbow of colors, a kaleidoscope spin,
Where every odd pairing just might be a win.

Bananas in pajamas dancing with flair,
Juggling their futures without a care.
In the land of the wacky, ideas take flight,
As the sun sets with sparkles, oh what a sight!

A sandwich is flying, it must be on break,
With lettuce and pickle, oh what a mistake!
But laughter erupts as it lands with a flop,
In this vibrant tomorrow, the silliness won't stop.

So here's to the dreams that strut without shame,
In a world full of wonders, we don't need a name.
With humor and giggles, together we'll sway,
To vibrant horizons, come dance in the fray.

The Language of Weaving

In a loom of mischief, we twist and we turn,
Words tangle like yarn, oh the lessons we learn.
A joke on the side, a pun here and there,
Laughs weave around us, like bread with no bear.

Knots turned to giggles, tangles to cheer,
Each slip of a stitch brings the laughter near.
With a wink and a winker, we craft quite a tale,
As the fabric of fun wraps our ship like a sail.

A fabric of jests in hues loud and bright,
We don our creations, wear laughter with pride.
In the seams of our stories, joy finds its place,
With the language of weaving, we tackle the space.

So gather your yarns, let's spin and unite,
With threads of humor that dance in the light.
In the art of creating and sharing the cheer,
We find in our weaving a world we hold dear.

Shadows of the New Day

The rooster crows at six, what a sound,
Yet, my coffee's lost, never to be found.
A sock on the floor, a key in the stew,
Who needs a map when chaos is new?

Birds scatter crumbs from the sky above,
While cats chase shadows, a game they love.
I step on a Lego, and dance with pride,
What a way to greet the bright morning tide!

Jumpy rabbits hop, as if in a race,
The dog joins in, making a funny face.
Here's to new starts and the giggles they bring,
Let's join in the laughter; let's see what life swings!

With a grin on my face, off to work I go,
Waving to clouds that put on a show.
Life's silly parade, I've a seat on the float,
Oh, the memories we'll weave in this merry boat!

Mosaic of What's to Come

A puzzle of plans fills the morning air,
With jigsaw thoughts strewn everywhere.
I can't find my shoes, what a curious way,
To start an adventure at the break of day!

Fridge magnets dance, a colorful crew,
Each promising meals that are fresh, not blue.
I mix up my lunch with the sock drawer's stash,
Meals that may fly, but they'll always be brash!

Clouds drift like marshmallows, fat and so sweet,
While squirrels hold meetings with nuts for a treat.
A traffic jam forms for a turtle so slow,
Oh, what a day, let the good vibes flow!

In the chaos of life, joy's quietly spun,
A tapestry rich with laughter and fun.
With silly mistakes that we know we can mend,
Let's weave this mosaic, on that we depend!

Delicate Connections

I bagged up my hopes in a crinkled brown sack,
But they fell out the hole, now there's no turning back.
With giggles they scatter, like butterflies free,
Each one a reminder of what could be me!

My phone's lost its mind; it buzzes like mad,
A message from the cat, that cheeky lad!
He claims to have secrets, to share with the dog,
In a world where hot chocolate now blends with fog.

The moon plays in shadows, but it's such a tease,
A matchmaker for dreams, with uncanny ease.
With socks still mismatched and hair askew,
This dance of connection is vibrant and true!

So let's frolic through life as if in a race,
With laughter our GPS, it guides with good grace.
Sticky notes yell "Follow!" on each page we roam,
In delicate connections, we find our way home!

Patterns of Tomorrow

The laundry spins tales that make little sense,
With shirts dancing cheekily, no need for pretense.
Each sock holds a secret, a whimsical plea,
While my cat sits triumphant atop a tall tree.

A calendar flips, and the days swirl with cheer,
When each new adventure is greeted with beer!
I trip on the mat, and land flat on my face,
But giggles erupt, I'm still in the race!

The world is a canvas of colors so bright,
Where even the smallest things bring great delight.
A paint-splattered spoon offers up quite the view,
Creating wild patterns, a whimsical crew!

So here's to the moments, the silly, the grand,
That weave into patterns, where laughter is planned.
For each day's a joke, a playful charade,
Let's brighten tomorrow, let's never be swayed!

Tapestry of the Unwritten

In the loom of dreams, I spin a yarn,
A sock with holes, oh what a charm!
My cat's the weaver, she pulls a strand,
    Chasing her tail, a silly band.

I stitch a future, just for fun,
With mismatched buttons, we've already won.
A quilt of laughter, stitched with cheer,
A cozy blanket, we hold most dear.

My neighbor's dog barks a silly tune,
In perfect harmony with the afternoon.
While picking threads from the cosmic bag,
I can't help but laugh; my pants are a rag.

So here's to the fabric of zany dreams,
Woven with giggles and outrageous schemes!
We'll wear our quirks, a vibrant display,
As we dance through life, come what may!

Sparks of Tomorrow

In a paradox lands where time takes a trip,
I've got mismatched socks, what a stylish slip!
With a hop, skip, and a playful prance,
I plan my adventures, in a retro dance.

An oven timer dings, dinner's on fire,
But laughter's the spice that I truly desire.
With a dash of chaos, and a sprinkle of cheer,
Tomorrow's a stage, let's give a cheer!

A chicken in sneakers? Oh, what a sight!
Ready for the races, it's a true delight.
With feathers flying and laughter within,
The spark of the moment, let the fun begin!

So here's to the mayhem, the joy and the glee,
Awakening visions, as wild as can be.
Grab your fork and knife, let's feast on the day,
In the banquet of tomorrow, we'll giggle away!

Threads of Faith

I found a spool of hope, rolled on the floor,
With a silly grin, I opened the door.
In walked a squirrel with a tiny cape,
Shouting, "Let's frolic, do you like grape?"

A tapestry wild, with colors galore,
Kaleidoscope dreams, who could ask for more?
With stitches of whimsy, I patched my heart,
Creating a masterpiece, a true work of art.

Forks and spoons become our silly swords,
As we battle the broccoli, defending our hoards!
With a flick of the wrist and a wink of the eye,
We'll craft a banquet that's fit for the sky.

So, come join my quest through laughter and cheer,
In our whimsical world, there's nothing to fear.
With stitches and giggles, we weave our tale,
In the tapestry of life, let's set sail!

The Seamstress's Vision

With a needle and thread, I dream my way,
Stitching nonsense in a whimsical display.
A pair of pants that fit like a hug,
Only if you're shaped like a friendly bug!

I measured my thoughts with a ruler of fun,
Creating a dress that sparkles like sun.
With polka dots dancing, and stripes all around,
Fashion's a circus where laughter is found.

My scissors snip ideas, one after the next,
A patchwork of giggles, what a perplexed!
As I twirl and I whirl, the fabric takes flight,
Turning boring moments into pure delight.

So grab your tools, let's sew up some cheer,
Here's to the visions that never adhere!
With joy in our hearts, let's make something bright,
In the realm of the seamstress, laughter ignites!

Weaving the Future's Fabric

In the loom of time, we splice a joke,
Hilarious patterns begin to evoke.
Spinning yarn with a wink and a grin,
Each loop is a giggle, let's dive right in!

Future's tapestry, quite a delight,
We patch up mishaps, with all of our might.
Socks and odd mittens, mixed colors and flair,
Who knew mismatched laundry could take us somewhere?

With each silly stitch, a new tale unfolds,
Knots of confusion, but brave hearts so bold.
We'll weave through the chaos, make laughter a thread,
Dancing with whimsy, no reason for dread!

So let's twist and twirl, in loopy delight,
Creating our future, ill-fated but bright.
A fabric of giggles, our fates interlace,
In the quilt of our lives, we each find our place!

Stitches of a New Dawn

Morning arrives with a playful grin,
Socks on our hands and a dance to begin.
The sun's a comedian, shining so bright,
Telling us jokes in the soft, golden light.

With needles for wands, we craft our own fate,
Each stitch a chuckle, we dance and we wait.
The fabric of life is a patchwork so fine,
Mixed laughs and odd shapes, all perfectly aligned.

The dawn whispers tales of absurdity's charm,
With each crazy stitch, we cause laughter, no harm.
We're here to create a ridiculous mess,
Each knot in our plans turns to humor, not stress!

From dawn until dusk, we'll twist and we'll weave,
In this wild adventure, we won't take our leave.
So gather your laughter, let's fashion the way,
With stitches of joy, we'll brighten the day!

Tapestry of Dreams Yet to Unravel

In the attic of dreams, we gather the thread,
Knitting together the things left unsaid.
Laughter's the twine that holds us so tight,
Creating a yarn that dances in light.

Each dream that we weave comes wrapped in a jest,
A patch full of giggles, it's simply the best.
A cape made of wishes, with pockets of cheer,
Let's wear it with pride, as we draw near.

Unravel the past with a chuckle or two,
Stitching the future, just me and you!
With spoonfuls of humor, we mix and we blend,
A tapestry formed; our laughter won't end.

So let's pull at the yarn, see where it goes,
In this fabric of life, hilarity flows.
Creating each day with a wink and a nod,
We're all part of a quilt, forever odd!

Echoes of Forthcoming Whispers

In the wind of tomorrow, whispers collide,
Witty remarks and laughter abide.
The future is chuckling, it's quite the surprise,
Tickling our ears with hilarious cries.

With echoes of whimsy and laughter galore,
We embrace the absurdity, always wanting more.
Silly ideas gather, weaving their spell,
Crafting our moments, like stories to tell.

So let's listen closely, each giggle a clue,
To secrets of joy that are waiting for you.
With threads spun of humor and fun in between,
We'll stitch up our futures with laughter unseen.

As the whispers take form, we twirl and we spin,
In this dance of delight, let the madness begin!
The echoes of laughter, forever they'll soar,
In this crazy quilt life, we'll always adore!

The Stitching of Infinite Possibilities

In a world full of socks, lost and confused,
I stitch up adventures, I'm happily bruised.
With buttons that giggle, and sequins that dance,
I'll wear mismatched dreams, give chaos a chance.

Each patch tells a story, each knot is a laugh,
My quirkiness blooms like a colorful scarf.
As I sew my new future, I trip on a seam,
But it's all in good fun—who needs endless gleam?

Needles may jab; I'll take it in stride,
For laughter's my fabric; it's worn with great pride.
Socks on the ceiling, my hats made of cheese,
In this zany life, I'm the master of tease.

So let's grab our yarns, let the laughter unroll,
With each stitch I make, I'm completing my goal.
In a funny old quilt, all tangled but bright,
I'm stitching the nonsense with sheer delight.

Silken Hues of New Beginnings

A chopstick parade in my bowl of old stew,
Says, 'What's next for dinner? How about you?'
As colors collide like a jester's attire,
Each spoonful an art piece, delightfully dire.

With ribbons of laughter and bursts of surprise,
I swirl through the kitchen, an artist on high.
My spatula sings as it dances along,
To the symphony played by a pot's bubbling song.

In the canvas of dinner, each flavor's a cheer,
As mismatched ingredients make everyone near.
So let's mix the chaos, let's savor the game,
In this feast so absurd, we're all culinary fame!

With every big bite, new journeys unfurl,
Silken hues wrapping our worlds in a swirl.
The laughter, the flavors, forever entwined,
New beginnings await in this banquet designed.

The Loom of Unfolding Tomorrows

A cat on my thread spool, spins quite the tale,
As I weave my next venture, she frolics with hail.
Each loop tells a secret, each knot grips a jest,
While I dream of the future, she takes a well-deserved rest.

The colors are blurring; it's quite the display,
I'm stitching the nonsense in a fun, crazy way.
With laughter like glitter and joy like a breeze,
I craft my tomorrows with giggles and ease.

Fluffy clouds dance by, all puffy and bright,
As I pull on the yarn and take off in flight.
In this land of the silly, where chuckles abound,
I'm weaving together the weirdness I've found.

So let's roll out the fabric, let the magic ignite,
With each silly stitch, we'll bring dreams to light.
Tomorrow is waiting, with quirks to explore,
A tapestry of laughter, forever in store!

Threads of Fate and Fortune

With a wand made of licorice, fate twirls in delight,
Spinning tales of wild fortunes that take to the flight.
A bubblegum horizon awaits my next dare,
With mischief and whimsy, I float through the air.

My fortune's a mystery, unraveling fast,
In a cauldron of giggles, I mix up the cast.
A rabbit with style, wearing shades and a hat,
Says, 'Choose your own future—let's start with a spat!'

As I'm sewing with jelly, confusion unfolds,
Each fortune cookie whispers the strangest of golds.
With every smart stitch, I'm embracing the rare,
In a tapestry sprinkled with whimsy and flair.

So let your own needle take aim at the wreck,
For even the wildest will sparkle with beck.
Fate's threads are all tangled; it's part of the plan,
To create a concoction of silliness, man!

Weaving New Stories

In a loom of laughter, we spin our dreams,
Each color a giggle, or so it seems.
With a snip and a stitch, we craft our fate,
A patchwork of chaos, oh isn't it great!

We tie up the past with a ribbon of cheer,
Dancing on strings that tickle the ear.
With memes as our fabric, and banter our thread,
We create with our folly, and laughter instead.

An Unseen Fabric

Invisible fibers, they wiggle and sway,
Mischief and mayhem, in a comical play.
One tickles the grandmas, another the pets,
While plotting new pranks, oh, what fun begets!

A tangle of joys, like a cat in the yarn,
We weave in good humor, no cause for alarm.
With laughter as glue, we keep us all tight,
In this whimsical quilt, everything feels right.

Bridging the Future

With a hop and a skip, we build our fair bridge,
Crafted from giggles, held up by a ridge.
Each plank a good pun, each beam a bright smile,
Connecting our dreams, let's walk for a while!

Jumping from here to that questionable shore,
Finding new jokes where the wild chuckles roar.
With our hearts intertwined, we'll dance and we'll play,
Sharing our jokes, come what may!

Echos in the Weft

In the fabric of time, echoes do ring,
The past throws us quirks, what joy they bring!
With each twist and turn, the laughter resounds,
As we strut through the stitches, in folly we're crowned.

Who knew life could be such a pun-filled charade?
With each woven tale, another joke is made.
From the tapestry spun, in giggles we nest,
In this fabric of laughter, we are truly blessed.

Crossing Borders of Time

A squirrel in a top hat, just zoomed down the lane,
With a pocket full of acorns, he offers me his grain.
He juggles clocks and calendars, with such a cheeky grin,

Saying, "Time is just a jump rope, come on, let's begin!"

The cactus dressed in velvet, speaks softly of the sun,
"I time travel for picnics, and man, it's so much fun!"
The grasshoppers are gossiping, with gossip just for kicks,

They claim they saw a snail that can do the cha-cha tricks!

A ladybug in sunglasses, is booking flights for bees,
"We're off to see the rainbow, just as soon as we seize!"
The caterpillars are knitting, unique scarves for a show,
They'll strut down with their laughter, making time twirl slow.

Yet as we skip through ages, with laughter that is bright,
A wise old owl reminds us, "You can't grasp the night!"
So we bounce through all the seasons, exchanging silly rhymes,
With giggles that will echo, across the fields of time.

Soft Beginnings

In a land made of marshmallows, where giggles fill the air,
A duckling wears a beret, saying, "Life isn't so rare!"
It dances on a teeter-totter, with a friend made of lace,
With every squishy bounce, they pull silly smiles on their face.

The tulips are debating, which color's quite the best,
But a jolly tree stump shouts, "Just wear a floral vest!"
They frolic in the starlight, with cupcakes in their hands,
Sharing dreams of ice cream castles and glittery wonderlands.

A bumblebee named Bobble bobbles through a cheer,
He's singing to the flowers, "Come out and join the sphere!"
With rhythm in their petals, the daisies sway and hum,
While the fireflies do a conga, calling everyone to come!

And as the moonlight tickles, all critters in their beds,
The dreams know no restrictions, just giggles in their heads.
So join the soft beginnings, where nothing's ever wrong,
With magic in our laughter, we always will belong.

Weave of Innovation

A toaster tap dances, with bread as his best mate,
Cooking up ideas, while singing 'bout fate!
He winks at all the waffles, who giggle at the show,
"We're inventing new treats; come join the doughy flow!"

Meanwhile, a light bulb twinkles, with sparks in every flick,
Reading books on solar power, he's learning every trick.
He'll light up the entire park, with gadgets made of glow,
While the ducks are running circuits, to see just how they flow!

A piano plays charades, with notes that bounce around,
He claims he's got a plan, to turn sound into the ground.
So they build a rainbow bridge, from harmony to cheer,
Connecting every daydream, to bring the future near!

And as the laughter rises, like bubbles in a pot,
A whirlwind of inventions, is all that they have thought.
So let's embrace the chaos, let laughter take its form,
In this weave of innovation, where giggles are the norm.

Sketches of the Future

A doodle on a napkin, claims to sketch the skies,
With a star drawn as a puppy, and clouds that wear bow ties.
It giggles as it glances, at comets turning loops,
Saying, "In the future, we'll teach fish to wear boots!"

A time machine made of crayons, and jellybean engines,
Is racing toward tomorrow, avoiding silly tensions.
The bouncy castle sunsets, send shadows swinging wide,
Filled with giggling giraffes, just bouncing with their pride!

A rhyming robot robot, sings tunes of yesterday,
While painting with the freckles, that light up in the spray.

It blasts joyful emotions, in colors oh-so-bright,
Saying, "Sketches of forever, are just giggles in the night!"

So let's doodle all our visions, with crayons full of fun,
Creating happy futures, where innovation runs.
With each silly little sketch, we hope to craft and play,
A canvas full of laughter, on this whimsical buffet.

Cadence of Uncharted Journeys

In the land of mismatched socks,
Where ducks wear hats and dance on rocks,
Each step's a giggle, each turn a grin,
The path is a riddle, let the laughs begin.

With shoes on backward, we strut and sway,
Chasing the sun, come what may,
The map's a doodle, the compass spins,
Who needs direction when fun begins?

A sandwich sings, a pickle prances,
In this wild world, laughter enhances,
We'll twirl around trees and leap over streams,
While lost in the silly of our wild dreams.

So join this trek of joyful delight,
With sparkles and giggles, we'll take flight,
For every mishap, we'll make a cheer,
In the game of life, it's laughter we steer.

Spectrum of Potential Awaits

Colors are popping, a rainbow's at play,
Jellybeans jumping in a wacky way,
A parrot in pajamas sings silly tunes,
As giggles explode like bright, happy balloons.

The sun wears shades, and the moon's in a hat,
A dancing bear plays a chitchat with a cat,
In this carnival of dreams, we skip and we hop,
Potential is vast, and we'd never stop.

With ice cream wishes and sprinkles of cheer,
Every moment is brighter, with no room for fear,
We'll paint our future with daisies and smiles,
In the vibrancy bustling, let's stay for a while.

So grab a balloon, let's float and explore,
For the world is our playground, a giggle galore,
With laughter as fuel, we'll rise like the sun,
In this spectrum of life, we'll dance and have fun.

The Fabric of What Lies Ahead

A patchwork of dreams in a quilt that we weave,
With polka-dots and stripes that make us believe,
The stitches of laughter are bright and bold,
Creating a story that never grows old.

With every snip and a silly string pull,
We craft a narrative that's wonderfully full,
Llamas in tutus prance down the lane,
As we stitch together our joy and our pain.

Navigating the chaos with quirky designs,
With sequins and sparkles, life brightly shines,
A fabric of whimsies, so cozy and grand,
We wrap ourselves warmly in joy's soft hand.

Let's twirl in this tapestry, giggle with glee,
For tomorrow's adventures are wild, just like we,
With each thread of laughter, we'll craft what's ahead,
In the quilt of our lives, forever we'll spread.

Vibrant Shades of Tomorrow's Canvas

Splashing hue on the canvas, oh what a sight,
With blueberry moons and marshmallow light,
A cat in a sombrero struts with flair,
While bubbles of laughter float high in the air.

The brushes are dancing, each stroke is a tease,
As gummy bears giggle on edible breeze,
In the carnival colors of what's yet to be,
We'll paint our adventures, wild and carefree.

With swirls of imagination, we dream and we dive,
In this playful palette, we come alive,
A canvas of wishes, a masterpiece grand,
The future is waiting, let's give it a hand.

So hold up your brush, splash joy with each hue,
For the world's our gallery, let's craft something new,
In vibrant shades, we'll dance and we'll sing,
For the laughter we share is the sweetest of things.

Looms of Destiny

In the grand old loom of fate,
A cat sat down, when it was late.
It danced on yarn, a yarn-filled spree,
Said, "I'm the weaver, can't you see?"

The clock struck twelve, the threads did twirl,
With every twist, they gave a whirl.
A chicken crowed, it thought it wise,
To knit a hat—oh what a surprise!

A squirrel scampered with a plan,
To stitch a suit for the tall man.
He said, "This fabric is quite a chore,
But I'll wear it well, I won't be a bore!"

In looms of laughter, we find our dream,
Spinning tales that often beam.
With every knot, we twist and turn,
In giggles and glee, we always learn.

Fabric of Sunrise

The sun comes up, a big ol' pie,
Woven clouds fluff like cotton high.
Coffee brews in colors so bold,
While toast pops up, a sight to behold.

The rooster sings, what a funny thing,
With feathers bright, he starts to swing.
As eggs do scramble, they dance and cheer,
A breakfast show, come gather near!

Pancakes pirouette on syrup streams,
Whipped cream mountains hiding dreams.
With forks as planes, we scrape and scoop,
In a fabric of joy, we all loop-de-loop.

A rainbow stretches, oh so wide,
In this morning's fabric, we all glide.
With giggles shared, we weave delight,
Each sunrise stitch feels just so right.

Interlaced Visions

In the land of dreams where socks unite,
One lost its pair but stayed in flight.
It twirled and spun, a dervish mad,
Claiming it's the coolest sock we've had!

An artist sneezed, paint flew around,
Creating chaos without a sound.
Colors mingled, laughed and played,
A vibrant mess, a splash parade!

Two mismatched gloves found a dance,
In winter's chill, they took a chance.
One claimed, "I'm stylish, can't deny,"
The other just said, "Well, at least I try!"

In interlaced visions, we find our cheer,
Wandering wild, we hold them dear.
Each stitch a laugh, each knot a dream,
In whimsical worlds, we always beam.

The Next Shore

We sailed to shores of jellybeans,
Where gummy bears dance in colorful scenes.
Seas of soda, waves of cheer,
What a delight, we all do steer!

A crab in shades, quite a style,
Waved hello with a crafty smile.
He said, "Join me for a snack or two,
I promise you, they're all brand new!"

A pirate parrot squawked with glee,
"Treasure's here, just follow me!"
But all it found were socks and hats,
In this crazy land, even rats wear spats!

On the next shore, we pitch our dreams,
With laughter and fun, nothing's as it seems.
Every moment, an adventure in store,
We joke and giggle, always wanting more.

Patterns of the Unseen Horizon

In boxes of dreams we sometimes forget,
Like socks in the dryer, they form quite a pet.
A mix of ambitions, a hop and a skip,
While llamas in tutus plan their next trip.

In gardens of giggles, the daisies arise,
With hats made of sunshine, they plot and devise.
The moon takes a nap, laughing softly at fate,
As jellybeans argue on how to debate.

With marshmallows dancing on clouds made of cream,
Every sprinkle of laughter is part of our dream.
A piñata of wishes swings high from the tree,
While penguins in tuxes form a conga with glee.

So gather your chuckles, your quirks and your cheer,
For every silly moment, a memory's near.
In patterns of nonsense, our hearts intertwine,
Each giggle a promise of futures that shine.

A Tangle of Aspirations

In a bag of ideas, they wrestle and twirl,
Like kittens in yarn, giving chaos a whirl.
Each hope comes with hiccups, quite proud of their stance,
While elephants juggle, creating a dance.

Tangled up ambitions take turns in the light,
With shadows that giggle, you'll find quite a sight.
Fish wear their hats as they swim through the air,
And otters on surfboards are happy to share.

With ice cream that sings, and cookies that cheer,
Our wishes hop madly, they're ready, my dear.
A tumble of triumphs, a splash of delight,
As skunks in tuxedos dance into the night.

So gather your fancies in baskets of fun,
With laughter as fuel, we'll always outrun.
In tangles of madness, our futures will gleam,
Each giggle a step towards our wildest dream.

Echoing Footprints of the Future

In shoes made of jelly, we stomp through the day,
With giggles and wiggles, we bounce on our way.
Each step is a riddle, a joke on the ground,
As squirrels run for office, election profound.

Echoes of chuckles ring through the tall trees,
As raccoons hold court with a side of cheese.
Their plans to invade the next pizza parade,
While rubber ducks wonder if they're getting paid.

Cartwheels of laughter roll out on the grass,
As butterflies argue on who's got the sass.
Footprints of fables wake dreams from their nap,
With donut-shaped clouds mapping out our next map.

In echoes of chaos, our futures will frolic,
Each giggle a spark amidst all that's symbolic.
So put on your shoes and let's dance through the haze,
For joy is a journey we savor always.

Embroidered Promises in Time

In fabrics of nonsense, we stitch up our dreams,
With needles of laughter, we plot and we scheme.
Each thread is a whisper, each knot a bright cheer,
While popcorn kernels plan a parade by the pier.

With sequins of sunshine, we patch up the night,
As owls in tuxedos take wing with delight.
They dive into puddles of jellyfish glow,
Creating a splash while embarking on show.

In quilts of our wishes, we cozy up tight,
While crickets compose songs to serenade light.
With buttons of giggles adorning the seams,
Our future is woven from sparkles and beams.

So dance through the fabric, embrace every line,
For every stitch whispers, you're destined to shine.
In promises crafted from laughter and rhyme,
We'll cherish the wonders of this merry time.

Weaving Light into Shadows

In a closet, I found a sock,
Dancing alone, made my heart rock.
It spun and twirled, a real wild sight,
Claiming it wove the stars at night.

Behind the couch, a rumble of fate,
Dust bunnies plotting their grand escape.
They whisper plans for a world anew,
In waltzing pairs, they just might break through.

A cat joined in with a sassy prance,
Tail in the air, oh, what a chance!
To weave through shadows, with glitter and flair,
Casting their giggles everywhere!

Laughing lanterns bobbing around,
Under my bed, more jokes abound.
Whimsical tales spun out of fear,
In this funny dance, let joy adhere!

Forms Yet to Take Shape

A pancake flips, oh what a sight,
Wishing to be a flying kite.
With maple syrup as its glue,
It dreams of skies so wide and blue.

Tomorrow's cake, a tower so tall,
Hoping to rise, but it might just fall.
Eggs and flour, a comedic twist,
Wait, where's my chef? Oh, here's a fist!

Pasta plans to become a snake,
Wiggling and jiggling, oh for heaven's sake!
But only if a sauce would help,
Alas, it just melts like a happy yelp!

Mismatched socks, eager with hope,
Wishing to elope with a stylish rope.
In the dance of fate, they'll take their chance,
And spin in circles, a wild romance!

The Fabric of Change

A duck in a hat, what's that about?
Quacking its way through a lively rout.
With feathers of wisdom, it rules the pond,
Promising magic, of which we're all fond.

The moths in my closet plot their escape,
Hoping to wear my favorite cape.
A fashion show of clumsy delight,
Who knew the dark could be so bright?

In the village, the elders complain,
About changing times, a light-hearted bane.
Yet butter on toast still stays the same,
As we all giggle and play this game.

The fabric of life, sewn with pure glee,
In each rip and stitch, there's a memory.
So let's embrace all that's kookily strange,
As we laugh together at the fabric of change!

Tomorrow's Loom

I woke up to a squirrel in a coat,
Debating if nuts were worth the vote.
It grabbed my toast, with a furry grin,
Promising joy if I just let it in.

The clock struck twelve, oh what a mess,
Pajamas still on, I must confess.
A fashion faux pas or a daring dream?
The bed's a runway, or so it would seem.

Clouds overhead are flossing their teeth,
Giggling down at our world beneath.
They whisper secrets of silly things,
Check out the new style that tomorrow brings!

In the sphere of chaos, laughter blooms,
Wrapping us tight in tomorrow's looms.
With joy and whimsy, we stitch our fate,
In a tapestry bright, it's never too late!

www.ingramcontent.com/pod-product-compliance
Lightning Source LLC
Chambersburg PA
CBHW060116230426
43661CB00003B/202